TIKI BLUE

A Poetic Journey
of
Life After Loss

Author
Greg West

PipStones

PipStones Publishing
P.O. Box 4507
Fort Walton Beach, Florida 32549
www.pipstones.com

Tiki Blue: A Poetic Journey of Life After Loss
Copyright ©2025, PipStones, LLC.

Author: Greg West

Editors: Abigail Turner, Deborah Hoffman, and Elizabeth Omoh
Cover Design: Robert Sauber

Copyright ©2025; Published in 2025

Library of Congress Control Number: 2025921097
ISBN-13: 979-8-9932579-0-7, Paperback
ISBN-13: 979-8-9932579-1-4, Hardback (Bl/Wh)
ISBN-13: 979-8-9932579-3-8, Hardback (Color)
ISBN-13: 979-8-9932579-2-1, Ebook

For Worldwide Distribution.
Printed in The United States of America.

Letter
from the
Publisher

"And the two shall be as one..."

I struggled after the passing of my husband—a marriage of almost fifty-five years. In that "oneness," the person you were no longer exists. Thoughts and memories are all that remain.

Thank you, Greg West, for sending your manuscript with a humble inquiry written on an orange sticky note. My answer to your question is yes: your writings would be of value to others.

My prayer for those who read this book is that you will be touched by Greg's messages in different seasons after the loss of someone so close to you. This book is a rare gift from a guy who open-heartedly has shared his thoughts and feelings.

P.S.
Thanks, Greg, for the fifty-dollar bill
that was attached to the note too.
Haha.

Deborah Hoffman
Co-Founder, PipStones Publishing

Dedication

This book is dedicated to my wife, Tiki Renee Blue.

What I had to lose to be able to write these words... was you.

May 1, 1962 - March 22, 2021

Memorial Ceremony Link:

https://vimeo.com/529799108

"My Morning Walk With Tiki"

For a handful of years now I have gone on a morning walk. In that quiet time after Tiki's passing, I often listened to these songs; ones that remind me of her or my situation. So, I refer to these walks as "My Morning Walk With Tiki."

I'm sharing these with you because these are the melodies and tunes that helped me through some days and touched my heart and my life.

These songs are a few of the thirty-five on a special playlist. Feel free to take a listen...

Tell Your Heart to Beat Again by Danny Gokey

One More Day by Diamond Rio

Scars in Heaven by Casting Crowns

I'll Follow the Sun by The Beatles

Everybody Hurts by R.E.M.

If Tomorrow Never Comes by Garth Brooks

The Hurt & the Healer by MercyMe

Table of Contents

Introduction

It's Monday morning, 7:00 a.m. on March 22, 2021, and my phone rings. The voice on the other end says, "We lost her." I asked what he was talking about, and he adds, "We lost Tiki."

At that moment, my whole life fell apart. Thirty-one years, three months, and five days of marriage to Tiki suddenly and unexpectedly came to an end. But the reality of it was that the struggle to keep going without her had just begun, and this was only the **"First Day."**

Maybe your story is different—but is the pain any less familiar?

This collection is for those who know that kind of ache—the kind that lingers in quiet moments and sneaks up without warning. Do you still lose your breath when a song plays? Does your heart skip a beat at a scent, a scene, a movie, **"Thoughts,"** or a memory that suddenly surfaces?

It happens to me all the time.

All of my writings began with one of these feelings that, for whatever reason, touched me. As you will see, I write from many different places during my travels. I would stop whatever I was doing at the moment and jot it down in my iPhone notes. For the most part, they only took fifteen to thirty minutes to complete. I didn't even know the title until I had finished scripting them.

Everyone processes grief in different ways and within different time frames. It took me two years before I started writing about **"The Past"** and looking toward the future. To be honest, I had no idea I would be writing a book someday. I was only recording these feelings and thoughts as they came to me. I found that I could go back and read them repeatedly to help me understand where I was in my grieving process. I could also see if I was getting anywhere close to returning to some semblance of a normal life.

I have shared some of these writings with friends and family, especially ones that were inspired by them or poems that were about them. The very special people I shared with are the ones who have **"Been There."** Sometimes, the written word to a person who understands grieving is more meaningful than a phone call. I've been told that it "really hits home," and speaks to the soul.

This book is a compilation of poems, journal entries, and prose—written across various travels, seasons, and turning points in my life. As you read, maybe it's a single word, a line, or an entire piece that resonates with you. Even if one part of this collection encourages you or speaks to your journey, then its purpose has been fulfilled.

SEASON 1:

June 2023 - August 2023

Friendship Seasons

Friendships are like the four main seasons,
Put into your life for many reasons.

SPRING, when friendships bloom.
SUMMER, when friendships grow.
FALL, when friendships wither.
WINTER, when friendships hide.

Not all friendships last all seasons—
Again, they stop for many reasons.
Some last for only one,
Some last for several,
Some last forever.

No matter how long,
They all have their purpose.
No matter which season,
In which they appear.
And how long they stay,
Always be grateful,
For you were blessed to have them here.

Which of these four seasons have you shared?
Which of these seasons have you shown you cared?

All four seasons need someone.

June 5, 2023

**This is the first thing I wrote in
poetic form, before I started
"dating" my writings.**

It was almost two months' worth of text
coming to life.

June 10, 2023

I don't want anybody crying for me.
I want to cry for myself.

June 15, 2023

Thoughts on the plane back to
Costa Rica from London.

The hardest part of leaving is coming back
without Tiki. My heart gets very heavy, and I
can't breathe at times. It will take a day or two to
get my mind and heart back up. It's been over two
years, and nothing has really changed how I feel
about losing her. I don't know if it ever will.
So many things every day remind me of her,
of us, and I doubt that anything could ever
change that. I travel all the time now to
keep busy and not get sad.

I sit alone at the airport now as many people pass by with someone, and I wonder why she left me.

Stool at the Bar

Having dinner alone,
No more tables for two.
Just as well,
No one to talk to.

The voice you once heard is no longer there,
That's why there will be an empty chair.

So when I see at the bar an empty stool,
That's where I'll be;
Dinner with me.

June 18, 2023

Frankfurt, London, UK at Great Thai Dinner

I wrote this poem on the plane from Frankfurt to London. Then, I had a great Thai dinner in London. I reserved a seat at the bar, but they gave me a "two-top" instead.

Trip in the Motorhome

I flew to Houston to visit Brianna (our daughter), and Gena (our granddaughter). Then, I spent four days with Becca at her ranch. I had dinner with her. And then I had dinner with Becca, Brianna, and Gena. I saw George and Renee, Leland (our son), Sophia and Penny (our granddaughter). I also saw Pat and Patricia (Tiki's sister), and Janice (Tiki's mom).

I flew to Sacramento and stayed three days with Mark and Allyson. It was a great three days, and I played the piano again for the first time in probably ten years. It was a good feeling. I flew to Portland to visit with Sean and Aubrey (my niece), Penny, Mara, and Sadie for three days. It also was a great visit. I got in the motorhome and started driving through Oregon. I was headed to Denver to see Robin (my niece).

What a beautiful drive it was through Oregon and Idaho. It was a five-hour drive through the Grand Tetons, and it was absolutely gorgeous! I woke up early and drove another twelve hours into Denver. I spent another three nights with John and Robin, and I enjoyed my visit with them. Then, I flew to Alaska to visit Dave (my brother) and Deb. Another great time was had. We flew the plane twice over glaciers, and I even got to help smoke their salmon. After that, I flew back to Denver for two nights with John and Robin. I picked up Becca and Karla at Denver International Airport and started the best nine days I had in two and a half years.

The trip was an awakening. I realized what I had lost, and what I may want again. I learned so much by being with Becca, but I also cried some more. It was some of the best times and the most beautiful scenery in those nine days. I considered it a blessing in disguise for me. I dropped them off at Phoenix airport and drove twenty straight hours back to Houston. I then visited with Leland and Sophia, and Penny (their baby). I also got to hold and feed her. It made me sad that Tiki was not there to do the same. I spent the night at the ranch with George and Renee, and had to take care of business before going back to Costa Rica. My August traveling ventures ended with a plane ride back to Candelilla in Costa Rica.

July-August 2023

I took a trip in the motorhome.

August 29, 2023

I have so much regret and am very sad that I was not by her side to hold her when she passed.

August 29, 2023

Today, I let Becca go without trying to share my situation so she can focus on her own recovery.

August 30, 2023

Someone had encouraged me to take a yoga class, so it was my first day. I felt positive about the experience and will continue to take private lessons.

Season 2:

September 2023

Two Seasons

Thank you so much
For the two seasons.
Why they stopped?
I don't know the reasons.

Never opened up
To one with the same.
I am very sure
That I am to blame.

I know that we shared,
I know that we cared.
We opened our hearts,
We opened our lives.

And it did me so good—
You'll never know why.
Not ashamed to cry
And let it all go.

The comfort was there
When we needed to share.
Our losses are so great,
Our hearts, they do ache.

But to lose a friend,
Seems twice as hard.
It's an empty space,
They are hard to replace.

So few who understand;
They've never been there,
So why should they share?
It was great while it lasted,
To know someone was there,
When we both needed to share.

But the seasons do change,
And they come to an end.

September 9, 2023

**I'm not looking for someone who loves.
I'm looking for someone who cares.**

September 12, 2023
Two Seasons was written on this date.

"H"

There's a time in one's life,
When we all have to choose.
What is important,
And what we can lose.

It's never so easy,
You do have a choice.
Times will be hard,
So listen to your own voice.

You've made the decision,
And it wasn't that hard.
Someone needs you,
Someone who's scarred.

Giving all that you have,
No matter the cost.
Less time with your friends,
But they are not lost.

Life is so precious,
And also so fragile.
You have God by your side,
And He's in your heart,
And that's the best and perfect start.

The journey is long,
But you are so strong.
It's day-to-day,
And minute to minute.
With no hesitation,
You are now deep within it.

Smiles and hugs,
Are free for the asking,
But giving them out,
Is so everlasting.

September 17, 2023

I wrote this to Becca, who was caring for and mentoring a young lady through a difficult time in her life. Even though Becca had several things going on (including the sudden loss of her husband), she dropped everything and gave the young lady 100% of her time and efforts.

A Fun Day

Find something beautiful,
And try it on.
Buy something cute,
While having some fun.

Grab a good seat,
And something to eat.
Maybe it's sweet—
Talking is neat
With that special someone.

Take time to breathe,
And cherish the moment.
Have a fun day.
There's lots more to come.

Written just for you, "H."
From Becca's friend, Greg.

September 18, 2023

**I wrote this to "H," the young lady
who Becca was mentoring.**

When I want to drift away,
I let my music play.
The special words,
They carry me somewhere.
I don't choose, and I don't care.
Might be to places I have been,
Maybe to ones I'll never see again.

They may precipitate some tears,
Might reveal some hidden fears,
Perhaps squeeze out a sideways smile,
But only for a little while.

Occasionally, I will share,
With someone who really has been there.
Oh, these special words,
Might make me sad or comfort me.
The secret of the special words, you see,
Is that they are special words, only to me.

September 18, 2023

**I wrote this on the plane flying to
San Miguel, Mexico, by myself.**

It Is What It Is

It will only be ten days,
Ten days to do what?
To sit and think of why?
It only takes these long hard ten
For reality to really sink in.
But nothing I do,
Will change what is through,
Even if I try.

At first, I shed tears,
And thoughts of past years.
What a life I've made in it too.
Then I say to myself,
"It is what it is."
There's nothing that I can do.

Go out, I say,
And have some fun,
Go out, I say,
And soak up the sun.

Stop counting the days,
Not going by faster.
Day ten and no news,
So what does it matter?

I know they are wrong,
l believe I am strong,
Because I have God,
And it is what it is.
More days in my path,
Too much I vow not to miss.

September 26, 2023

**This is day ten, and I'm still waiting
on my biopsy results.**

Therapy's Over

This was the first message I read,
Trying to get things straight in my head.
Where we were, with what we lost—
You had yours, and I had mine,
But the difference was the time.

Times have changed,
Much is rearranged.
All for the better, now it will be,
Asking just, "How are you?"
Is there anything new?

Once in a while, a song may be sent,
Or a really nice shared picture,
To make both our lives feel much richer.

September 27, 2023

**After I wrote this, I read the daily message in
Jesus Calling—God Wink.**

Not These Thoughts

I have a friend who is dying,
That is why I'm crying.
Will see him the next day,
But only to say,
You are not alone.
I'm on the same path,
We are all headed home.
If I don't do what they say—

It has taken so long,
After all, they could still be wrong.
For the first time in a while,
With no reason to smile.
I'm sitting here, drinking,
Trying to get drunk,
And block out the thinking.
Definitely not good to get caught,
Giving myself over to this vein of thought.

At least—not these thoughts.

September 28, 2023

**It's Friday night and I'm sitting
at home at Candelilla in Costa Rica.**

A Church of Music

A church with only music,
It softens my heart.
It eases my mind,
But that's not the only part—
Some tears I may find,
And it gives me great peace.
It helps me to smile,
Often brings me to my knees.

It relieves my pain,
To sing to the King who reigns.
As I ask for forgiveness.
Much emotion to show.
As it makes me shout
I believe, I believe, and I know...

It all leads to prayer,
No sermons to share,
And nothing to fear,
So give me the music,
That's why I am here.

September 30, 2023 at 1:00 am

**It's late for me, and I'm listening
to Christian music.**

SEASON 3:

October 2023

No One Here

No one here to be with me,
Even if we disagree.
No one here to watch me sleep,
Or when it's time for me to weep.

No one here to hold my hand,
And help me walk across the sand.
No one here to have a fight,
Even though she was usually right.

No one here to watch sunsets,
While I say there are no regrets.
No one here to ride with me,
The car is empty as can be.

No one here to show that smile,
Yes, it's been a long, long while.
No one here to say I love you,
All these words, they do ring true.

October 4, 2023

**I wrote this sitting on the deck at
Candelilla in Costa Rica.**

Moving Forward

My time has arrived,
It's amazing how I've survived,
To open my heart,
And reveal a new start.

I decided to go,
On a trip with the two.
But I never knew,
What to expect,
Or how I'd react.
A new view of my past,
How long could it last?

I saw what I'd been missing.
It was mostly me not listening.
Looking forward to new places,
And meeting new faces.
Something different and new,
Like the day I met you.
Where it all began,
I am starting again.

Where this journey leads me,
I'll just wait and see,
But I'll always remember,
You'll be here with me.

October 5, 2023

**A note to myself about my
Tiki and two special ladies.**

Someone?

Waiting for someone to come into my life,
Not necessarily to be my wife.
A companion for sure,
But what's the allure?

With no certain plans,
And time on my hands.
Maybe for travels,
We'll see what unravels.

Able to leave at the drop of a hat,
Very few people get to do that.
There's a world to see,
And would like someone with me.

Will she find me, or I find her?
It all depends on where we were.
A look in the eye, and a quick glance.
Is either willing to take a chance?

October 9, 2023

**This is written as a follow-up to
"Moving Forward"
— a new day with new thoughts.**

Life's Trials

Finally got some really good news—
To get me out of these down-and-out blues.
Don't know why it took so long,
But now I know there's nothing really wrong.

Now going back to making my plans—
To drive my motorhome around these vast lands,
To fly on a plane and go anywhere.
Where it may land, I do not much care.

A lot of things for me to see,
Not so sure that it will be just me.
It's a brand new and hope-filled day,
And I will pray that things go my way.
Just looking for some beautiful smiles,
Through many of life's unending trials.

October 17, 2023

**I wrote this a few days after letting the results
of the biopsy sink in. Trials are bumps and
roadblocks in our otherwise smooth life journey.**

When one speaks to your heart and soul,
You hope they know where you have been,
And also where you want to go.

They only know if you open up.
They only know if they will listen.
They only know if they've "been there."
Oh, so many think they know.

They try to tell you how to feel,
Or tell you what to do,
But then it goes back to the few,
The ones that know and have a clue.
So if you really have "been there,"
Reach out and show how much you care.

October 19, 2023

**Note to self: I don't know why these things just
keep coming to me so easily. The past few writings
have been about me, but this one is about others.
Maybe someone, somewhere, will read it
someday and do something
they've never done.**

Delight

It's nine at night,
And time for bed.
It's time for her
To scratch my head.
Her on the left,
And me on the right.
One last kiss,
And we say goodnight.

With earplugs in,
And book in hand,
She is now ready
For fantasy land.
Her hand on my head,
I'm out in a few.
But she will keep reading,
How long? No one knew.

Those were her worlds,
Where she would go,
To be part of them,
And no one would know.
Her mind is at peace.
Her thoughts she would keep.
They belong to her,
As she drifts off to sleep.

This is how it was,
For over thirty-one years.
The left side now empty,
And sometimes brings tears.

But the thought of her joy,
In reading each night,
Brings a smile to my face,
And great delight.

Tiki reading at her favorite place:
The pool at Candelilla

October 22, 2023

I woke up this morning and wrote this
while lying on the left side of our bed.

SEASON 4:

November 2023

Seventy-Five

Well, I made it to seventy-five,
And I am still alive.
It's been a good day,
So what can I say?

Started by waking,
And that's a good way.
Talked to the kids,
And they sang me a song.

Got a massage,
And time to relax,
Even nibbled on some birthday snacks.
Now time for dinner,
With brother and friends.

It's been a good day,
As we toast to the age.
My time is not done.
Looking forward to Seventy-Five plus One.

November 2, 2023

**I wrote this to myself while I was in
Destin, Florida for my 75th birthday.**

Dancing with "E"

It really was to no surprise,
When I looked into your eyes,
As you asked me up to dance,
I said no, then took a chance.

Of course it had been many years,
And it was honestly one of my fears.
You took me out onto the floor,
I was not afraid anymore.

I'd just met someone who's new,
And had some fun with a nice dance too.
It for sure had been a while,
But it brought me to a smile,
Thank you for the question in asking.
Because I wouldn't have been dancing.

November 2, 2023

Written for Elizabeth.

David

Here's the man who brings a smile,
He leaves it with us for a while.
He knows not how it comes to him,
But I'm sure it comes within a whim.

David likes to make you smile,
To bring back laughter for a while.
Doesn't matter where he is,
Always seems to fit right in.
Different voices and different faces,
He takes you to such different places.

What a pleasure and a blessing,
Always leaves you with some guessing,
For who he is and where he's been.
He is David.
He's my friend.

Tracy & David

November 2, 2023

About my friend, David.

Memories vs. Future

When do these two turn loose and go their separate ways? Memories of the past, not wanting to leave them behind. Visions of the future, wondering what you will find. These two battle each other in your mind. The memories you already have and the future you can't see, but it is out there somewhere. Places you've been vs. places you will be going. People you already know vs. people you will meet. Events of the past vs. happenings of the future. The memories of the past will usually win the battle until you decide to keep them in a special place. You need to start a new season in your life, filled with new memories.

Emerald Coast - Destin, Florida

November 4, 2023
I wrote this on the beach this evening in Destin, Florida, after sharing my past and future with someone I just met at lunch. They also shared their story with me.

Trip Thru Time

A trip thru time,
When you were mine.
Here together,
But not forever.

I came thru early,
And you a little later.
Somehow we met,
For a nice long time.
But it went so quick,
That trip thru time.

Now you've left early,
And I'll leave later,
On this trip thru time.

Time is forever,
We'll meet again,
I'll never say never,
On our trip thru time.

November 12, 2023

**This came to me as I was driving on the
Natchez Trace Parkway in Tennessee.**

Feeling The Ring

It's been on a finger for seventy-seven years:
Forty-two on my father's, thirty-one on mine,
now four on my son's.

But there are times
I feel it's still there,
On my ring finger
Like it never left there.

My heart skips a beat,
And my breath goes away,
I reach for that finger,
Just to see if it's there.

Well, I know that it's not.
It's just an odd feeling,
Memories of her,
And the life that we were living.

I feel it must be her saying,
"I'm still with you, Love."

November 13, 2023

**I wrote this early in morning.
A feeling that has been happening for a long time.**

  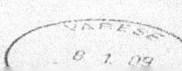 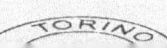

Silence

What is it like to be alone?
No one is there when you get home.
Just silence hanging in the air,
No one is there to show you care.

Walls all covered with the past,
Just how long will this silence last?
Prepare a meal for just one,
Wash the one dish and now you're done.

Music plays to pass the time,
Pour yourself a glass of wine.
Sit in silence and watch a sunset,
Sometimes this may help you forget.

Time alone, it goes so slow,
For those of you who do not know.
Minutes are like hours,
And hours are like days.

Now the night has come,
And it is time to rest.
You crawl back into that empty bed,
And lay down your weary head.
Once again, the silence I dread.

November 17, 2023

**One thought early this morning came to me,
and I finished the thought—
What is it like to be alone?**

Having people around
ls what I've found,
Changes your thoughts in many ways,
Especially on those special days.

Family and friends,
Is where it begins,
Some you've just met,
But at least don't forget,
The ones that you know,
From a long time ago.

Some are not here,
It may bring a tear,
With lots of laughter,
It's what they are after.

To see them prepare,
Has been very rare,
And to be included,
That's to what I've alluded.
Times have changed,
My life rearranged.
Thank you, my friends,
It's not where this ends.

November 23, 2023

**Thanksgiving day at Becca's ranch with her family
and friends. For the first time in three years,
I spent this holiday with just friends.**

Give It To Me

If you see trouble,
In someone I know.
Give it to me,
I'll take the blow.
If hard times do come,
I can take some.
Give it to me,
And set them free.
If someone's in pain,
I have nothing to gain.
Give it to me,
And let them be.
These things and more,
Will cut to the core.
Give them all to me,
And I will thank thee.

November 24, 2023

**I wrote this the morning after Jake spoke
to me about what was on his heart last night.
It did us some good.
Refer to the Book of Jake 1:1. Haha**

I Wish It Was Me

Music is playing.
Two at their table.
Arm on the shoulder.
A whisper in the ear.
I see them smile.
I see them touch.
Even a kiss.
I see "the look."
I hear the laughter.
Someone special for sure,
To say what's new,
And how are you?
Are they married?
Are they putting on the moves?
Is it true,
Or just BS?
It doesn't matter,
That much to me.
Just like to see,
Those little sparks fly.
Though I am free,
It's still only me.
It's taken some time,
To clear my mind.
To set it straight,
With help from friends.
And strangers too,
Now I wish that it was me with you.

November 25, 2023

**At 9:45 pm, I'm sitting in a jazz bar in
Houston and seeing all the couples in the place.**

SEASON 5:

December 2023

Again

You left me here all alone,
And now you're at the throne.
Now you're there face to face,
You are in that special place.

Where you wanted, time to dance,
Now you have your dancing chance.
It's where you wanted to always be,
Even though you had to leave me.

They say I'll see your face again,
But your face was one of a gem.
I know I'll see you there, my dear.
It's just a point in time.

Yes it makes me happier,
To know that you are there to shine.
So save for me a certain place,
To see your beautiful shining face.

December 1 & 2, 2023
**I had a thought on the drive back from
San Jose, Costa Rica, yesterday and wrote it down.
I don't know why, but today I finished that thought.**

What's To Come

How I see me
In twenty twenty three:
I'm seventy-five,
And still alive,
And I don't feel my age,
Trying to turn the page,
And write a new chapter,
Here's what I am after.

It's hard to cope,
But I still have hope,
That someone's there,
And we can share,
In my last days,
In many ways.

Things to see,
And be with me,
By my side,
Along for the ride.
Places to go,
We won't know,
Just where they are.
They could be far,
Or just sit at home,
Us two alone.

I'd like to know,
If she will show.
I know that it takes time,
And I am not in my prime.
The thing that I fear,
Is that she will never appear.

December 3, 2023 at 6:00 am
These are thoughts that cross my mind frequently
now that my future has taken a different
direction in the past several months.

First Day

You wish that day
Had never come.
That moment in time
When you lose someone.

You get the news,
But you choose,
To hope and pray,
That it's not true.

As you sit in disbelief,
Your mind slips off into grief.
The tears, they flow
Like a waterfall.

The screams of pain,
You can't refrain.
The sound of silence
On deaf ears fall.

Your mind goes blank,
As you sit and stare.
You ask again,
Is this a dream?

You're not aware
Of who is there.
And at that moment,
You don't really care.

Your body is numb,
You cannot rise.
It's hard to look
In peoples' eyes.

Time slows down,
As seconds pass.
How long will
This nightmare last?

After a while,
Reality sets in.
You ask yourself,
How long has it been?

Nighttime comes,
And you cannot sleep.
Your heart just aches,
And your eyes still weep.

It's just day one.
There's more to come.

December 4, 2023

**I wrote this knowing that a special friend
has "that day" coming up. This is what I remember
about my first day. I am sure that most of this
hits the memory of a lot of people.**

Thoughts

Thoughts passing
Through your head,
Some of them
Will make you dread.

Where you've been
From the start,
Some of them
May seek your heart.

Then they go
And take your breath,
It's all about
Life and death.

Some of them
Are very good,
They make you smile
As they should.

Some are sad
And may bring tears,
As you think
Of those past years.

These things you think
They belong to you,
And some of them
Are all brand new.

All this happens
Almost every day,
In some small form
To your dismay.

In between these
Thoughts of yours,
It's back to the present
To open new doors.

December 10, 2023 at 6:00 am

**Just thinking about how I feel when a
new or past thought comes over me.**

Hole in my Heart

I have special friends,
But none in my heart,
To fill in that hole,
For that fresh start.

That part of my life,
Just seems so bare,
Wondering if someone,
Will ever be there.

To fill in the hole,
That needs repair,
Someone who knows,
And someone who cares.

Out in my travels,
Never long in one place.
Odds I won't meet,
That smiling new face.

You see, I've been told,
To slow myself down,
And plant my feet,
Firmly in only one town.

But this I can't do.
It was pretty good advice,
And not that I didn't,
Think on it twice.

The world is wide open,
And there's too much to see.
So for now in my travels,
It will still be just me.

December 12, 2023

**This is just how I feel at times in Costa Rica,
or in my motorhome, or on a plane
traveling somewhere.**

Here are some words
About a special man.
Just imagine
If you can.
He's still here with you.
He's been in your heart.
A special memory from the start.

For those who knew
What he'd been through.
It was his drive
That kept him alive.

From the time he awoke
He'd tell a joke.
You'd be in stitches
Might pee in your britches.

He was a businessman
But foremost a family man.
A daughter and two sons
Were his special ones.
His love for these three
Was a very special **KEY**.

He mostly didn't know
What to say
So he told a joke
On her wedding day.

He had three granddaughters
And three grandsons
They were also special ones.

And you surely can't hide
That angel by his side.
She even pulled from her pocket
To feed him his last chocolate.

Melissa was a dear
For Murray's last year.
He lived a long life
And in the end
With family at his side,
He peacefully passed,
And those not there,
Were present in prayer.

You'll always remember
This man's face.
His heart and soul
Were full of **LOVE** and **GRACE**.

Murray & Janet (Murray's Daughter)

December 13, 2023

This is written for my "adopted family" and friends about a very special man. These are definitions that I gathered while writing this:
KEY: of paramount or crucial importance
LOVE: an intense feeling of deep affection
GRACE: to honor or credit someone by one's presence.

Day 365

How is this day
Unique from the rest?
From that very first day
To a year of sunsets?
Is this day merely a test?
No one knows, it's only you,
But you'll need some help,
To see all this through.

You may ask yourself,
What really has changed,
Since your daily life,
Has been rearranged?

All these days in between,
Most days were very hard,
Some a little better,
Since that time your life's been scarred.

Some you wish,
Weren't there at all.
The days seem long,
When plans shatter and fall.

What else could go wrong?
But a light comes and then you see.
Remember the beautiful ones?
That's how they all should be.

Some bad dreams,
And thoughts in your mind.
You wish they were not there,
And were another kind.

Some of these memories
Will even make you smile,
Trying to keep you happy
If only for a while.

Sometimes you want
To run and hide,
With no one there
By your side.

Many sleepless nights,
As you shed those tears,
To cry yourself to sleep,
And ask again how many years?

There's always the what-ifs
That play in your mind.
If doing was done different,
What would you now find?
Or if some small things
Didn't happen at all?

Would I have received
That telephone call?
What if I'd been there?
Would this day still be here?
Would things have been different,
Through this very difficult, long-lasting year?

All of these things,
And much, much more,
Come back on this day,
You wonder what for?

They carry you back
To that very first day,
And thoughts in between,
As your feelings give way.

You have to keep,
In the back of your mind,
With tomorrow's sunrise,
What will you find?

No backing up time.
It's day three sixty-six,
And there are some things,
You just cannot fix.

December 14, 2023

**I wrote this about a special friend who was getting
ready to have her Day 365. Not to make her sad, but
these are memories of our past. I was not writing
back then when it all happened.**

Different Thoughts

A thought just came into my mind,
If someone appears at my door.
My past writings you will find,
But these I feel should be no more.

They are too full of sorrow,
And too much of the past.
Now there is a new tomorrow,
Let's hope that it will last.

Should be writing for that reason,
Some new thoughts of hope.
It should be for a newer season,
While I'm still trying to cope.

It took a while to get here,
For others not so long.
But let's get one thing clear,
Some of us are not quite as strong.

When and if that day appears,
Whenever that may be.
It may erase some tears and fears.
I'll have to wait and see.

December 18, 2023

I wrote this on the airplane from Costa Rica to Georgetown, Guyana. I was thinking that all my writings should not always be so sad. I would like those who read them to feel a sense of hope.

Holidays

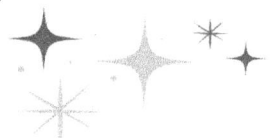
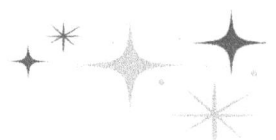

Haven't done the holidays,
Always wanted to be alone.
Found excuses in many ways,
For me to stay at home.

I know that family is always first,
Didn't want to bring them down.
But always thought the worst of it,
Was them having me around.

December 19, 2023

A Prayer for Becca

Becca,
Wanted to let you know,
My heart is with you today.
I know you might feel low,
But the best I can do is pray.

This prayer is here to say,
Lord, give her peace of mind.
As she makes it through this day,
No telling what she'll find.

Help her remember those days,
That put a smile on her face.
And show her many ways,
For new things to take place.

You already know her needs,
She can always rely on you.
For you to plant those seeds,
To help her make it through.

Becca,
This day may feel so long,
As time slips away.
But God knows you are strong,
And tomorrow is a brand new day.

December 19, 2023

**I wrote this for my friend, Becca, as
Day 365 passes by with the loss of Michael.**

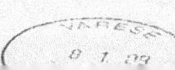

Christmas Songs

It's now Christmas Day,
Trying to be of good cheer.
And as the music plays,
Certain songs do bring drops of tears.

Your life is incomplete,
As you give a big sigh.
And your heart skips a beat,
Wiping that tear from your eye.

As the songs play on,
You remember good times.
But those are all gone,
As your heart realigns.

You thought you'd be okay,
But it's back to here and now.
On this first Christmas holiday,
You'll get through the ache somehow.

It's the family by your side,
The way they show they care.
Their love they cannot hide,
Helping your heart to repair.

Then as your ears give way,
To the music once more.
Your mind just drifts away,
To these songs you can't ignore.

December 25, 2023

**I wrote this on my first Christmas that I spent
with others since Tiki left. I was in Guyana
with Brianna, Karel, and Gena.**

Season 6:

January 2024 - February 2024

First Christmas

Christmas with the three;
First one in three years,
With Karel, Gena, and Brie,
And some New Year's cheers.

These have been the best of days,
In a very long, long time.
I cannot even count the ways,
With this family trio of mine.

Great to sit and talk,
And to laugh a lot.
Then go for a walk,
Almost forgot what I've got.

This time in Guyana,
It was worth the trip.
Spending time with Brianna,
Even enjoying a nip.

Each day has been fun,
Meeting their friends.
And a day in the sun,
Is how some days have begun.

And as these days,
Come to a close.
I think in many ways,
That's merely the way life goes.

Gena, Brianna, and Greg

January 3, 2024

It took me a few days to finish this poem.
Right now, I'm sitting at a restaurant
in Barbados, waiting for my lobster.
I'm at a loss for words sometimes.
Love you all – Dad

Sometimes my head hurts from self-talking to myself. I even ask myself too many questions. It often feels like I never have the right answers, and who can truly say if they are even correct? There is silence in the air, and my lips are not moving, but the thoughts keep coming one after another. I ask myself why things are the way they are, and have thoughts of the past and visions of the future. These two are colliding in my mind, and I'm wondering which one will survive.

As my eyes are looking quickly around, they are trying to distract my silent thoughts and give them a break. Sometimes this works, other times it doesn't. Sometimes I tell myself to just quit thinking.

January 4, 2024

**I wrote this while eating dinner alone on my first night in Barbados. Just my thoughts and me.
I'm not sure if this makes any sense,
but who cares if it doesn't?**

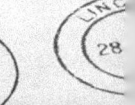

I see the waves in the distance and feel the cool breeze in my face. I see the tables in front of me with couples having dinner. There is soft music playing in the background. I see couples walking by on the street, and I wonder where they are going—surely somewhere to have some fun.

I came here on a whim, and Barbados has been great. But that's the way my life is now; just going with the flow. Yet, there is still an empty chair on the other side of the table. For now, things seem to only happen when they are meant to be.

January 6, 2024

This is just a short note while eating dinner in Barbados. This is how I feel at this moment in time.

The Next Table

I'm having dinner with my son (Leland), daughter-in-law (Sophia), and granddaughter (Penny). Our time together is never enough. But we make sure to take what we can get, since each of us has our separate lives.

I'm observing two young ladies at the table next to ours. They are having so much fun as if they have no cares in this world. Just watching them laugh and hug each other brings warmth to my heart to see that they each have a friend by their side. There are many smiles between the two of them.

I used to smile and laugh like them. But now I wonder why it's not me, and how every smile and the laughter I have now is almost all just pretend. Yet, it's still so nice to watch and see just how happy some people can be. I blessed their table and watched for their reactions. The glimmer in their eyes as they glanced around, trying to figure out who covered the bill, was priceless. Being able to give fills me with joy. As we left the place, a big smile spread across my face.

February 8, 2024

I just had a great dinner with Leland and Sophia after a long motorhome trip. I was able to bless someone this evening.

Songs

Listened to some songs,
That I didn't want to hear.
It's been a while,
Thought they'd bring a tear.

But to my surprise,
No tears came from my eyes.
I must be getting better,
Accepting how things are.

I cannot change the past,
I am in the here and now.
I'll take whatever comes,
I'm just blessed to be around.

February 13, 2024

**I wrote this on the plane from Houston
to San Miguel, Mexico, listening to
music on my iPhone.**

Special Friends

Exploring unknown places is much more enjoyable with a companion. You never know where you'll end up, and that uncertainty is what makes life exciting. You're sitting and sipping, chit-chatting, laughing, and just people watching. I'm with my friends and their friends, whom I just met, and I feel so blessed to be here. But sometimes you question why you are here because you sure didn't plan it. Sometimes, these are the best of times, not knowing what is to come. So, be thankful for your special friends who appear in your life.

February 17, 2024

I wrote this after a very memorable evening in San Miguel, Mexico, at Max's restaurant. I was with my friends, David and Tracy, and their friend, Laureano Brizuela (an Argentine singer and songwriter), and Max and his wife. It was late in the evening, and the restaurant was closed. We were the only ones there. We sat for hours catching up, and eating a great meal.

Faith Lost

She was my rock,
And now she's gone.
And I've lost my faith,
Don't know where it went.

She always kept it close,
Making sure I always knew.
That it was there for us,
Now it's nowhere to be found.

Where did the faith go?
Will I ever have it again?
If she were here with me,
She would say it never left.

Hard for me to believe,
That it will reappear.
She was the special one,
Who made sure I understood.

February 21, 2024

I listened to "My Morning Walk With Tiki" playlist on the flight back to Costa Rica, and was thinking about who and what I've lost. Coming back is always very hard the first few days. I keep busy to distract, but it always catches up with me.

SEASON 7:

March 2024

DAY 1096

It's now year three,
As my thoughts are of thee.
You're always on my mind,
So many things you've left behind.

I could not foresee,
That you'd be leaving me,
To be on my own,
Having to live life alone.

The silent memories in my mind,
Loved ones that you left behind.
The many lives that you have touched,
Many paintings that you have brushed.

Our two kids that you had raised,
I am sure they're still amazed,
You were the mom that they both needed,
That's why the two of them succeeded.

Always looking at some pictures,
And sometimes reading scriptures.
The Godly woman that I knew,
I'm who I am because of you.

I'm at the beach without you, my wife,
Where we all celebrated your special life.
I know you're with me and I am there,
So I will sit and say a prayer.

You were my one and only lover,
And my very special cover.
I'll always be thinking of you,
My lost love TIKI RENEE BLUE.

March 4, 2024

**I wrote this today because I can't get the
upcoming third anniversary of the loss of
Tiki off my mind. It seems just like yesterday.**

ME

Sometimes in a person's life,
Everyone fights a little strife.
Thinking that they want to be,
Anyone else rather than ME.

But me is the one,
And it's hard to run.
From what is within,
This body of skin.

Things aren't always the best,
Putting your life to the test.
Not liking what you see,
In this person I call me.

Things I'd like to change,
Some only to rearrange.
Thoughts run through my head,
Taking back things that I have said.

But who would that person be,
If I was not going to be me?
Looks like a very hard choice,
I'd have to listen to my voice.

But if I were to choose,
What things would I lose?
My soul and my heart,
Those I've had from the start?

So after much thought,
I just think it's a NOT!
I always want to be,
That person I call ME.

Greg in Istanbul

March 10, 2024

**I wrote this after reading the lyrics
to a song that a friend wrote.**

Tiki & Leland

Tiki & Brianna

It's now again that special day. I'm hoping you have a calm and peaceful one, knowing that I love you both. Wishing that she were here in our midst to hug, hold, and say, "I love you." But reality sets in, reminding us that she is not here. I'm thankful we do have all the memories of her from past years—trying to keep them in our minds so we can find and retrieve them when we want to go back in time.

Leland & Brianna
At Tiki's Memorial Service

March 22, 2024 at 12:35 a.m.

**A little note to Brianna and Leland about
this very special day in our lives.**

Peace of Mind

Today as I sit on the beach,
You're by my side but I can't reach
And touch the one I knew,
I'm here by myself without you.

The waves keep rolling in,
This beach where you have been.
You so much loved the sea,
I wish you were here with me.

It's so peaceful here and calm,
Sitting underneath this palm.
And with a gentle breeze,
I hear it touch the trees.

There are people walking by,
I'm sure they wonder why,
I'm sitting with your urn,
But it is not their concern.

There is music in the air,
From the speaker on my chair,
And sometimes there will be,
Only the sounds of the sea.

Memories keep coming to mind,
I don't know what I'll find.
But there's one thing I know,
I will never let them go.

Yes, I've shed some tears,
Because it's been three years.
But it also brought some smiles,
While going through these trials.

It's now time for me to go,
And just so you know,
I know I'll be alright,
I'll have peace of mind tonight.

Thinking of my daughter and my son.

At the memorial site of Tiki

March 22, 2024

**I wrote this while sitting all morning
at the beach in Costa Rica, where
we had Tiki's celebration.**

I'm walking down the path at the beach that I walked three years ago. It brings back so many memories that it makes my heart skip a beat. It seems like it was so long ago, yet it feels like only yesterday. I see it in my mind, but I would rather it not be there. Yet it will always be there to share with me alone. There is no one else here with me, except you in my mind and heart. It was a very special day here with family and friends. But now I am alone from that moment on. I always watch the video of that "special day" when I want to be near you—your Celebration of Life—the day you were washed away.

March 24, 2024

I wrote this today because I happened to be at the place where we celebrated your life in Costa Rica. I did not plan it, but it must have been meant to be. It worked out to be two days before the ceremony, but I believe it's better now than not at all.

SEASON 8:

April 2024

What do you see as they turn their head? They look into your eyes and flash you a big smile. As they walk away, it's as if they say, "I want to see you again, and now it's your call." But you don't know what else to do. The moment has passed, and you just do nothing. You just lost your chance to maybe meet someone or talk for a moment. So, in the future, you should never let that moment pass.

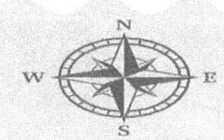

April 2, 2024

I just wrote this as thoughts passed through my mind after this happened to me.

I have to believe that there's more than just a dog to keep me company and help me stay sane. It's nice to have one around, but it's just not like having a woman. Dogs don't speak; they just lie on your lap, but a woman is there to help you speak your mind. Sometimes you're asking questions, and other times you're being asked questions. Sometimes there is just silence, but you know that she is there. They both like to be touched to know you are there. A glance in the eyes is a sign that they care. Even without speaking or having a touch, you know that your best friend is by your side. No matter which, it all comes down to what you want or need in your life.

April 7, 2024

I wrote this earlier in the morning, while sitting in a chair with Frank's dog, Gus, on my lap in Fair Oaks Ranch, Texas.

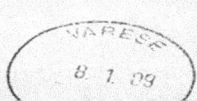

I'm a Traveling Man

If you think being on the road,
Or being on a plane,
And flying somewhere,
Will help you to forget,
You're most certainly wrong.
She told me it's a lonely curse,
But it's enticing to others,
I'm in between the two right now.

You see it's just me.
I'm still all alone.
It's just a way to pass the time,
Oh yes, there are the new places,
And maybe some new faces.

But it still comes down,
To there is no one around,
To share the new moments,
That I have just found.

I still call it running,
From what hurts so bad,
To stay on the move,
After all, what do I have to lose?

But this vagabond life,
Will certainly end.
When I find that someone,
To share life with again.

Or maybe or not,
I will continue the journey.
Step by step, I'm not in a hurry.

I'm a traveling man.

Traveling Excursions:

*Purchased Mercedes Sprinter Motorhome in June 2022.
*Took 7 different trips for a total of 24 weeks.
*Traveled over 40,000 miles.
*Visited 41 states in the United States.
*Traveled 10 plus days through Canada.
*Traveled throughout 19 different countries by sea and air.
*Several countries were visited multiple times.

April 13, 2024

**I wrote this after a special friend had
messaged me a note. It inspired me to
write something about my present lifestyle.**

Five Years

Five years of our lives,
Was a long time ago.
Had dinner tonight,
Just to say hello.

We both had laughs,
And lots to say,
Remembering the past,
Of those yesterdays.

And for some reason,
We went a separate way,
But to look at it now,
It all turned out okay.

We both made new families,
To love and be raised.
Who would have guessed,
We both would be blessed?

Now over the years,
How our lives have changed.
We still have our kids,
But the times have rearranged.

Both flying solo,
One with more years.
It is what it is,
No reason for tears.

Our lives are now different,
From those five in the past.
They were great years,
Weren't meant to last.

What's in our future,
We cannot be sure.
But now I know,
We both will endure.

April 19, 2024

I wrote this early this morning. I had dinner last evening with my first wife, Joyce, in Mesa, Arizona. It brought back a lot of memories, and I'm so glad we can still talk. Make sure you always cherish what you've had, even if things didn't work out as planned. Look at the good things that emerged afterward.

Mountain Drive

Gallup to Telluride,
With no one on the passenger side.
Telluride to Durango,
Both drives were so slow.

Three hundred and thirty miles,
Without any smiles.
Not a word was spoken,
And the silence was not broken.

The curves and the hills,
It gave me some thrills.
It made me feel alive,
I needed to survive.

And the beauty of it all,
Helped me to recall,
The trips that we've had,
Which made me very glad.

If I could do it again,
Although not sure when,
Or with whom would that be,
In that seat next to me?

Not sure if now it's needed,
Others have preceded.
They filled that empty seat,
And made my life complete.

It was a wonderful day,
And it turned out okay,
And what can I say?
Tomorrow is yet another day.

Loveland, Colorado

April 20, 2024

**I wrote this after a great long drive
through the Colorado mountains.
Just another day on the move.**

The Movie

It was just a movie
That I'd seen before.
But this time I couldn't
Watch it through anymore.

I got through some,
But it came to a place.
I had to turn it off,
As it crept in my space.

The space I'm in now
Is so different than then.
I don't want to fall back
To where I've once been.

I think that I've come
A very long way.
My life is so different
Since she went away.

I have to admit
That my mind will allow
These thoughts from the past,
Like what happened just now.

I know this will happen
As the days go by.
So all I can do
Is ask myself why.

April 22, 2024

**I wrote this late at night, watching a movie, "The Choice,"
on my phone in my motorhome in Taos, New Mexico. I
guess that sometimes you do or see something that takes
you back, and it makes you sad, and you
just don't want to go there.**

Alone or Not

Sometimes I still wonder
If I have room in my heart.
I may be out of love,
No space for a new start.

Each day I wake up
Thoughts come in my head.
Would I rather be alone,
Or have someone instead?

I'm ready for either,
Whatever comes to be.
It could be with someone,
Or it could just be me.

It's taken some time
For me to decide.
It's okay for someone
To be by my side.

I'm not in a hurry.
What will be will be.
You can't make it happen.
Life has no guarantee.

So I'll continue to travel.
Lots of places to see.
And maybe I'll find
Someone to be with me.

April 26, 2024

**I wrote this while in Santa Fe, New Mexico,
sitting alone in Jackie and Emma's home.**

A Minute in a Line

One minute of time
So what do you say
To a friend of a friend
While you're standing in line?

The loss you both had
One far longer than the other
The mention of their spirits
That the two of you feel.

Their spirits are there
And you have no clue
When they will appear
To flutter your heart.

To give you a sign
And just to remind
They're still with you
If only in your mind.

In so many ways
They are talking to you
To just let you know
The love that you had.

That minute in line
Went by so fast.
Who would have ever thought
You'd be talking about the past?

April 26, 2024
**I wrote this after meeting a friend of a friend,
Christina, in the drink line at an art opening in
Santa Fe, New Mexico. She lost the love of her life
also. Neither one of us was up for small talk. It
was better to talk about what was on our hearts.**

SEASON 9:

May 2024

Henry & Suzanne
Married May 26, 2024

I saw what the both of you sure had,
In San Miguel when I met you two.
It's something that made me certainly glad.
And that is when I undeniably knew.

You two sparkled and shined,
I saw the look in your eyes.
It helped to remind,
How sometimes we say goodbyes.

But you two are saying hello,
And this time it's for life.
As you say the words "to bestow,"
You'll make this woman your wife.

Sometimes it may get a bit rough,
Most times it will be fine.
You'll even live with each other's stuff,
Your lives are together by design.

Each sunrise is a different day,
Not like the one before.
So be careful in what you want to say,
And try to not keep score.

Make sure you say hello,
To each other every day.
This helps the marriage grow,
The one you said to honor and obey.

As the coming years pass by,
Much faster than they seem.
The days and hours how they fly,
Has this all been a dream?

The answer will be no.
Your hearts will never sway.
You watch your loving marriage grow,
Beyond your beautiful wedding day.

Henry & Suzanne

May 10, 2024
**I wrote this wedding card for the two of you
because store-bought ones are not what I
wanted to say. Also, because here in
Costa Rica, they are all in Spanish.
Haha!**

Where Are They?

There are times now and then,
But you never know exactly when.
You don't want to be alone,
And you feel like an unknown.

You always wonder who is there,
And if they really care.
That shouldn't cross your mind,
Good friends are hard to find.

They'll be there if need be,
No matter if it's a he or she.
They'll always have your heart,
Even if you're far apart.

Ones with whom you've shared,
They let you know they cared.
With tears you still can't hide,
Maybe some family by your side.

The silence can be deafening,
Or sometimes even refreshing.
But once in a while you fear,
Over things you didn't hear.

No one there to speak,
From those whom you seek.
Still wondering where they are,
Are they near or afar?

The emptiness inside,
Is always easy to hide.
You just have to give a smile,
Take a seat and wait a while.

May 12, 2024

**These thoughts have been on my mind for
the last few days, so I decided to write them down.**

Day-to-Day

It's now been three plus years,
And no one has appeared.
So what does that say to me,
This new life has no guarantee?

I've seen many new places.
And lots of new faces,
But no one special for me,
So that I might become a we.

I know the time that it takes,
To get over all the heartaches.
They say it's no reason to worry,
So I can't be in such a hurry.

But whoever's saying things to me,
I surely don't have to agree.
So now I am aware,
They may have never been there.

And in the blink of an eye,
I stop and wonder just why,
They try telling me what to do,
I might have a different view.

So I'll just go on my way,
Of living my day-to-day.
Forgetting all my fears,
As today just disappears.

May 12, 2024
**I was laying in bed late at night. There was just
more thoughts going through my head.
Sometimes it takes a while for them to come out.**

Touch & Speech

The things that went away,
Some are still not here today.
Most of them were small,
And some I can't recall.

But some of them I need,
To help me plant a new seed.
To enable me to get there,
I really need this pair.

Touch is number one,
And right now I have none.
No one to hold my hand.
Most people won't understand.

I need someone close,
And that's what's missing the most.
I'm living on my own.
Without you I feel alone.

Speech is number two,
Having no one to speak to.
My words just disappear
Into what seems to be thin air.

There is no answer back,
The words fall through the crack.
There's no one there who hears.
Will all of this last for years?

These two and many more,
Are what I had before.
But now they both are gone,
My future plans redrawn.

May 13, 2024

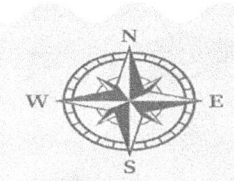

**I was thinking how important these two senses
are in a marriage, and how you lose both
with the loss of your spouse.**

P.S.:
**To be honest, I wasn't the greatest at either one,
and she would have been the
first to agree with me.**

Are You Hiding?

Don't let your sorrow
Ruin your next tomorrow.
What makes you feel
That today is not real?
Is it the hurt from the past?
How long will those feelings last?
Or is it only today
That's getting in your way?
If trying to let go
Is a lot harder than you know,
You have to look and see
All the possibilities.
Take a look around,
And something may be found.
You may never know when
Your new life could begin.
Time is on your side,
But have you even tried?
Get up and out of your chair,
And take yourself somewhere.
No matter where you go,
You just need to show,
That you have a life ahead,
There's nothing for you to dread.
So put a smile on your face,
And go to find a happy place.
You'll see there's more to life,
If you let go of your strife.
You have your special friends,
They could be where it begins.
You have them on your side,
So don't stay home and hide.

May 16, 2024
**I actually wrote this while driving to my biweekly massage in
Dominical, Costa Rica. I was speaking into my notes on the
iPhone, and yes, I know you're not supposed to be doing that.**

Little Red Heart

There are things that I did
To show I loved you.
As small as it seems,
It was a part of my dreams.

The mark on my wrist
After time had a new twist.
Some words that you spoke
Started out as a joke.

It got into my head,
Couldn't believe what you said.
It now had a new meaning,
And it was demeaning.

It was now causing pain,
And the mark couldn't remain.
Now my life has changed,
And my feelings reframed.

What was once said,
I need to get out of my head.
So I made it go away,
No longer on display.

Now I have a fresh start,
Without my little red heart.

May 17, 2024
**I wrote this about a special friend telling me their life story.
Only she knows what I just wrote about. Even though there is
great loss and pain in losing your spouse, you sometimes
remember the hurt that the two of you had along with the love.**

Random Thoughts

I've been writing all of these thoughts for nearly thirteen months to record what my life now brings. Things haven't gone exactly as I thought they would, but that's just the way it is. I've shared some of the writings with some family, friends, and even strangers I've met. I hope I've also been able to help them in their loss, but I'm not sure I was of much help at all. Some of the writings seem so depressing, and I wish they were not so sad. Sometimes I think to myself, *Are these words really about me?* And the answer is probably yes.

I can't have what I had, but at times I think I can. The past is in the past, and today is here and now.

I can't change where I was, but I can change where I am going. I've been writing for and about myself, while thinking I've been writing for others. Some of the writings evoke sadness, while some bring joy. Sometimes I think about not writing at all. I have to change my tune and outlook, so things will get better. I'll continue to travel to see the world around me as I believe that's where my future lies. Being by myself on the road, seeing this new life through a different pair of eyes. I am who I am and just want to be myself and have a happy heart. I know I've lost my faith, as it left with Tiki. The loss has left a big hole in my heart, and it has been hard to fill.

May 17, 2024

**These are just some random thoughts on
how I feel at this moment in my life.**

A Kiss

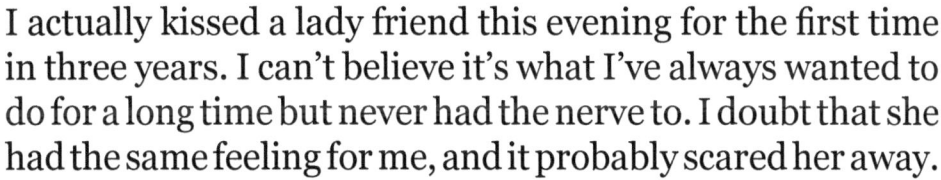

I actually kissed a lady friend this evening for the first time in three years. I can't believe it's what I've always wanted to do for a long time but never had the nerve to. I doubt that she had the same feeling for me, and it probably scared her away.

It's been so nice to learn about her life, who she was, and where she's been. I still remember the first time she came into my life. I was so scared, scarred, and vulnerable. I actually asked someone how to go about holding hands with someone. I felt like I was in high school again with a crush, not knowing where to begin. I think that when you experience a spark, you should just let it be and see if it ignites into a flame.

Maybe I should apologize to her for things I shouldn't have done. But if you never take that chance, odds are you'll never know what you may have missed. If I have offended her, I want to sincerely apologize and hope that I did not end our friendship.

May 20, 2024

It's a situation in my life that I hope will be for the better. Even if it isn't a step forward, it's a step that I would eventually have to take sometime in the future. I sent this to her.

This has been a good day,
And what can I say?
After watching all of them,
Wondering where they've been.

They seem to have no fears,
About the coming years.
They're enjoying the time that's here,
With their loved ones very near.

Watching them is fun,
Reminds me of things I've done.
Those years so long ago,
And how was I to know,
That I would end up here?
It made it very clear.
It's where I was supposed to be—
Here with only me.

May 24, 2024

I wrote this at a beach resort in Cartagena, Colombia, with Henry and Suzanne's young wedding party. I felt very privileged.

One-Hour Flight

When you start your day,
And there's no one near to say,
What's going on in your mind,
Who knows what you will find?

But things were going wrong,
That made the day very long,
I was not aware,
As I sat down in that chair.

But then she appears,
And the reason is unclear.
She has something to say,
The conversation is underway.

Small talk and some chatter,
The topic doesn't matter.
You talk about the now,
As short time will only allow.

You sit and wonder why,
Is it to make the time go by?
But soon after you start,
Both are talking from the heart.

Answering questions you are asked,
You both share from your pasts.
It brings out some smiles,
And even past trials.

Both have something to share,
Talking to someone is rare.
Someone is listening from behind,
But neither of us cares or minds.

It's a blessing that we met,
Someone I should never forget,
And it ended that night,
After only that one-hour flight.

May 28, 2024

I wrote this after Bailey befriended me and conversed with me on the flight from Nashville to Destin. You never know when someone will enter your life for a special reason, even if it's just for one hour.

The Point

Sometimes you'll be let down,
In your heart you'll have a frown,
From those that disappoint,
Or maybe you've missed the point.

It may not be as it seems,
Could it be only in your dreams,
That someone was really there,
And you thought they would care?

This could also be a test,
To see if it's really time to invest,
In a person who shut the door,
You've had that done before.

All will work out as it should,
And maybe you've misunderstood.
The intentions that you saw,
Were not there at all.

So don't let them enter your heart,
As you're looking for a fresh start.
Tomorrow is a new day,
And things may go your way.

So wake up with that smile,
That you haven't had in a while.
It's just been buried deep inside,
Now let the then and now collide.

Greg at Destin Harbor

May 30, 2024

**I'm just sitting in Destin,
and this happened to me.
I need to heed my own advice.
I'll see in the morning.**

SEASON 10:

June 2024 - August 2024

Not a Doll

She thinks I look like someone,
But I really look like no one.
It's just me in this shell,
That no one knows but me.

She had that pretty smile,
But then she left for a while,
And later on returned—
Came and stood next to me.

She asked a few questions
But already knew the answers.
She came pretty close,
It's like she knew me to a T.

She had eyes that pierced,
From my eyes to my heart.
Haven't had that feeling
In a very long time.

Saying our goodbyes,
Outside in the nighttime air—
We'd only just met,
It was an evening to not forget.

As she gave a final hug,
She whispered in my ear—
A thought no one has ever said,
"You're a doll," and I said, "I'm not."

June 14, 2024

**I wrote this today after a meeting and being
befriended by Christina on my last evening
in St. John's, Newfoundland.**

Things Unsaid

It was a moment of chance
When I caught that glance,
But I wasn't able
To get a seat at the table.

At the table I'm seeing
Is another human being.
She just happened to appear—
Wonder why she's here.

It is always very hard
To let down your guard,
And allow someone in,
Knowing where you've been.

But getting involved
Doesn't get that moment solved.
The many plans she had,
Are so hard to add.

You understand why,
And you get no reply.
So you let it go,
And leave the memory at hello.

There were things left unsaid,
You don't know what's really ahead.
And you ask yourself why—
It may not be your last goodbye.

June 17, 2024 at 4:30am

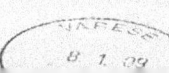

I wrote this sitting at the airport in St. John, Newfoundland. It was just some thoughts of someone I met and didn't really have a chance to get to know better.

Back in Costa Rica

When I come back,
I see what I have lacked.
The ones that I have met,
The few I can't forget.

My time is always short.
My feelings I must abort.
You see I don't stay,
And say what I want to say.

There have only been a few,
And if they only knew,
What that moment meant to me,
How it set my mind free.

It's so hard to forget the past,
Those thoughts that always last.
To try and let them go,
So no one will ever know.

These feelings deep inside,
I'll never be able to hide.
I know there's someone there,
Who will listen and won't care.

Short journeys here and there,
My feelings are unaware
Until a certain spark ignites,
And gives my heart delights.

But it's a good thing for me
That only I can see;
There are better times ahead
If I don't leave my thoughts unsaid.

View from the deck at Candelilla

June 27, 2024

**I wrote this to myself after returning
to Costa Rica from Newfoundland.**

The Unknown

It's still so strange,
With so much change
In my new life,
Since I lost my wife.

I go to places just to think,
Maybe sit down and have a drink.
I look around at all the faces—
It's the same in all the places.

I don't want to encroach.
I would rather they approach.
Very seldom I'm given that chance
For my feelings to advance.

No one ever wants to know
What really makes my mind go.
Of all the people and some places,
Only a few have left some traces.

But that's the way my life is now.
Maybe fate will not allow.
With all new journeys that I take,
Maybe I'm making a big mistake.

I can't seem to settle down.
I look and see what is around.
If that's the way my life should be,
I'll settle for myself just being with me.

So every day I'll wait and see
The new things in store for me.
Most of the time I am alone,
Just waiting for the unknown.

July 5, 2024

I wrote this back in Costa Rica. It's the way I feel at the moment and how my life is going. It's what someone shared and said of how I keep things bundled up inside of me.

Well, I'm traveling again and trying not to remember things from my past. I'm on a plane to a new place so that I won't have to deal with what I once had—things I have lost. Waking to new days to see what is there. It will always be something new, that I am sure. But is it false hope that something will appear in my life to bring about a change? One must believe that new things will emerge as their life takes a new direction. So, I will just take this new day and the next new tomorrow as an opportunity to be thankful that I have been blessed.

July 16, 2024

These are some thoughts on the flight from Seattle, Washington, to Anchorage, Alaska, to visit my brother Dave and his wife, Deb. This is basically how my life has gone for the last three and a half years. I've been blessed to visit some wonderful places during my travels.

Blue Chairs

Sitting on the blue chair,
Wondering why you're not here.
Was a very special place
Where I could see your face.

But now I have to imagine
That you are here with me.
It sometimes feels that you are.
Other times you seem so far.

Bringing back those memories,
Of when we were together.
Going back to the place,
That brings a smile to my face.

I am now in San Miguel,
And it makes my heart swell.
Sitting in this special blue chair,
Where we were so many times there.

You were trying to paint my face
Into your painting of this place.
You said that you were having trouble
And then you were gone in a double.

Your painting is on the wall,
It helps me to recall
The fun times we had shared,
While having breakfast in the blue chairs.

Greg in the Blue Chair
Unfinished Painting by Tiki

August 1, 2024

**I wrote this while once again sitting in a
blue chair at Cumpanio in San Miguel, Mexico,
where we always ate breakfast when we visited.**

There are moments in my life that I believe may never come around again or perhaps mark the start of something new. I try not to think that this could be the time. But as time goes by, I wonder if it wasn't meant to be. Is she not interested in me? I don't want to push, so maybe I should just let it go. There were one or two that could be special. But not like this one because there is a lot of mystery here. Yet she is so far away, and I'll probably never see her again. I tell myself time and time again that it's really so hard to find that special person. Just someone who cares and wants to be by my side. Telling all truths with nothing to hide. We all have our pains that stem from our pasts, but now should be the time for new beginnings in mind.

August 4, 2024

I wrote this in Houston, Texas, after watching a movie titled "Love again." It tugged at my heart and memories, both from my past and my current life.

Truth

Most of the time,
I like being alone,
Sitting by myself,
With only my thoughts as my own.

But some of them,
I wonder just why,
I'm sitting alone,
No one by my side.

It's not that I don't
Want someone near;
Speaking truth to myself
Is probably what I fear.

What do I really want
In my life ahead?
I don't really know,
Because it changes when I wake from my bed.

Places I go,
People I meet,
Things that I do,
Change the way that I think.

Afraid to commit,
Even to ask for a date—
The truth be told,
It scares the hell out of me as of late.

It's easier to just write
About me with my thoughts,
Rather than try to find
Someone who's worth a shot.

It's so much easier,
Just to be alone;
Me and my thoughts,
Peace and quiet at home.

But where is that home?
I travel so much.
Lying down my head,
In so many places I have touched.

So truth being spoken,
I think I'm still running
From what could be;
Being by myself with only me.

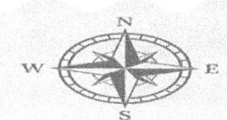

August 9, 2024

**I wrote this while wondering why things
in my life are what they are.**

Losing Again

It's not that I haven't found a woman whom I want to be with. It's that I haven't found a woman who wants to be with me. I see them every day in all shapes and forms, but they might as well be from another world. They can be so close, yet they seem so far away. They all have their own lives, and I wonder who they really are.

It's so much easier to just look and think of what could be. Why would anyone want to find out what's inside of me? Looking from afar is much safer than it seems—not having to share my inner thoughts and dreams. So, I just keep to myself with hardly any moves. My life is so much easier than having to lose someone again.

August 12, 2024

I wrote this one evening after a friend said he thought I would have found someone by now. It kind of hit a nerve with me, and I didn't take it well. Three and a half years doesn't really feel like a long time sometimes.

SEASON 11:

September 2024 - December 2024

No Laughter

It struck me as I sat
And watched her as she laughed.
It's something that I was missing,
As I was just reminiscing.

A little something that I'm after,
You see I've lost my laughter.
I see it in many places,
Watching it on other people's faces.

It's been a long while,
Since I've had a true smile.
And a laugh from the heart,
Like I forgot how to restart.

I need something to laugh about,
And that's why I am without.
The laughs that come from within,
Hope they will soon happen again.

September 12, 2024

I wrote this in Florida as I watched people laughing and smiling. It took me back to "Touch and Speech" that I wrote back in May. It's just another thing missing in my life these days.

Fred

Sitting there that night in a bar,
I always wondered who they are.
We lost him back in 2020,
But his friends around me are plenty.

Those who knew him from later years—
Thoughts that brought a few more tears—
But also brought some laughs,
Maybe he's here with us, perhaps?

I knew him when we were young,
When we were both among
Those ones just having fun.
Our lives had just begun.

But our lives went by so fast,
As our paths had seldom passed.
But there were those who filled in,
And became his next of kin.

A few times we got together,
Not to talk just about the weather,
But to recall our times that passed,
Future memories that would last.

It turned out to be a great night,
Even though we can't rewrite
How we all lost our friend,
And our lives would upend.

Fred in a shooting blind in Kerrville, Texas

September 21, 2024

I wrote this in Connecticut after a spur-of-the-moment
detour on my drive in New England. I was blessed to
finally meet Fred's close friends—the ones who
befriended him and took care of him.
I also saw his sister, Freda.
What a blessing!

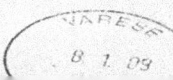

What Was Lost

I wish I had someone who stared into my eyes,
Like I saw her do a moment ago.
I see the smiles
And the love that they display,
As if to say I am here for you.

The beauty that you see within,
Is here for now and hopefully forever.
You're holding hands so I know you're close.
Don't ever let go of what you have,
Because you never know,
If it will be here tomorrow.

Having someone by your side,
Is the most important moment
In your life today.

September 28, 2024

I wrote this in Bar Harbor, Maine, sitting in a great little bar and watching a couple and wishing that I had that connection again.

I'm still running so fast, hoping my past won't catch me. I'm always going to new places and always in different directions. I'm hoping that I stay ahead and that it can't keep me in its sights. Sometimes it gets close, and momentary thoughts appear. At other times, it gets really close, and the thoughts linger for a while. Sometimes these thoughts are good ones, and at other times they bring me sadness.

Don't think you can always outrun it because it's always somewhere in your mind. You never know when and where it will show its face. It could be at that empty seat at a table, on a plane, driving down the highway, or even wake you from your sleep. The past can show up when you least expect it. Sometimes when it shows up, it's not that I have slowed down and let it catch me. I think it's just the past's way of wanting to remind me of what I had.

October 2, 2024

I scribbled down some notes a couple of days ago while driving in the Adirondacks. I put them down today.

Regrets

One definition of regret deals with loss,
And those who have it—come at a cost.

So many times the ones who treated you right,
Are the last to be there to help with your plight.

But you always need to be aware,
You never know who will appear and show they care.

October 26, 2024
**I wrote this after reading someone's
post on Facebook. Life is too short
to wake up with regrets.
"So, love the people who treat you right.
Forget about those who don't."
This is a quote that I saw on Facebook.
This is why I wrote this poem.**

New

How do you finally let go?
Not completely though.
But only just enough,
To make moments not so rough.

Sometimes you have to see,
That it's not only about me.
You have to look around,
At the people that you've found.

They're in your life for a reason,
If only for a short season.
So enjoy them while you can,
It's all part of God's plan.

What's meant to be will be,
Even though you may not see,
What and where your future lies,
Right before your very eyes.

So you take every new day,
Putting your old thoughts away.
Focusing only on what is new,
And new will take care of you.

October 29, 2024

I wrote this sitting in Destin, Florida, thinking about my just completed 7,000 mile motorhome trip. I was pondering the people I met, and wondered where I would be during the upcoming holidays. It's always a tough time of the year.

Last Night at B&B

Sitting at a table for two,
But only one without you,
Looking at everyone in sight,
You're not here with me tonight.

I know it's been a while,
Since I have seen your smile,
But just to let you know,
I still can't let you go.

You're always on my mind,
And it's awfully hard to find,
One that compares with you,
And I know this to be true.

It's not that I have tried,
To have someone by my side.
I still like to be alone,
Looking forward to the unknown.

November 9, 2024

**I wrote this at B&B Steakhouse in Houston.
It's where I come for dinner every time before I
return to Costa Rica. Sitting at a table for two with
an empty chair. Same thoughts every time. That's
just the way life has presented itself.**

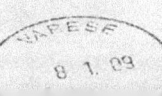

Hhh
Lots of options if you choose,
And you have nothing to lose,
Just a chance to be,
Somewhere with me.

No matter the place,
You'll never be able to erase,
This moment you shared,
With someone who is scared.

To let someone in,
From where I have been,
And find one who will share,
Because you know they care.

Just some time to forget,
What we both once had,
And enjoy ourselves.

November 13, 2024

My first unfinished work, hence the title Yy and Hhh. I wrote this after a great dinner with a wonderful lady who shared with me. I didn't finish or send it because I decided to leave well enough alone and let nature take its course.

"I Wish I Lived Your Life"

What do you say to
Someone who tells you
They wished they lived your life
Not knowing you have lost your wife?

Your life's not all that it seems.
They think you're living out your dreams,
But they are so unaware,
That they really don't want to care.

They must think it's all for fun,
But it's more like being on the run.
So time does not just stand still,
With your thoughts you try to fulfill.

They know not what they'd lose
If it's your lifestyle they would choose.
They don't know all the facts,
So how does one react?

It really touches your heart,
Since your life fell apart.
You know it's been a while,
So you simply show a smile.

December 13, 2024

I wrote this poem over the past several days in
Barbados. This is how I feel after meeting people,
and they ask me what I do. I tell them that I'm
retired and just travel. And sometimes
their next comment is,
"I wish I lived your life."

December 16, 2024

Dinner at The Naked Fisherman in St. Lucia.

A young newlywed couple from New Jersey
(Mike and Nicki) were sitting next to me,
and during our conversation, she used
almost the exact same words as the title
of this writing. I had to show it to them.

How do you get to ground zero? It's just a little ahead of where you currently stand in life. It's a big blank canvas, and it's all you can see. So, how do you begin to fill it in? You start anew by taking chances and looking at things differently—by exiting your norm and finding things you'd never expect to see or do. You have to speak your mind when placed in a situation you haven't been in for a while. After all, you have nothing to lose.

Look toward your future, no matter how far ahead it may seem. Are there things you will need to get your new life back to normal? This raises questions about what "normal" really means and also brings your past into consideration. The trick is, how do you get both of them to coexist in your mind? Life today seems to be a daily struggle because there is no normal. The past is in your mind, so when and where will that and normal meet? When will you find this place where you accept the past for what it was and your future for what it will be?

This is where you find your ground zero, with nowhere to go but up.

December 17, 2024

I wrote this sitting at home at Tikivibez (the new name for the Candelilla that John and Janet chose) in Costa Rica, one week after returning. The words ground zero popped into my head, and I wrote them down to figure out why, and these are the words that came out.

Silent Dinner

One of the things,
That this life brings,
Is silence at the table,
Because you are unable
To have a voice to answer,
And you just want to ask her.
But because she's not there,
Sitting in the other chair,
Not even to say,
How was your day?
It would fall on deaf ears,
As it has for years.

As you look around,
At those who have found,
The one with whom to share,
I hope they will always be there,
To be by their side
And not to be denied,
The love that they speak,
Is what we all seek.

December 18, 2024

**I wrote this in St. Lucia on my last night.
I sat at yet another dinner table for two
with one empty chair.**

Christmas Memories

As Christmas Day approaches,
Your mind receives in doses,
Of those loved ones from before,
As they are hard to ignore.

You start to remember the places,
And all of those faces,
Of the ones that were there,
And now you just compare.

What was then,
But what is now,
As you try to allow,
These next few days ahead,
As you keep your real thoughts unsaid.

And sometimes you really feel,
That at times it's not for real.
The one you've lost isn't here,
And now it's been another year.

As the Christmas music plays,
It again reminds you of those days.
When all of it was in good cheer,
And the one you loved was near.

But since your life has changed,
And even much is rearranged.
You know you'll be okay,
On this upcoming Christmas Day.

December 21, 2024

I wrote this one in Guyana, sitting at my daughter Brianna's house with some Christmas music playing. Some songs bring back memories of the past. But it's a blessing to be here in the now.

SEASON 12:

January 2025 - February 2025

This writing is about the new things that have happened to me in the last five days. It was the first time in four years that I had done this. First of all, it took a lot of nerve for me to ask a lady to travel with me. I was not sure how it really came about, but I'm so glad that it did. Over the past four years, it has only been an occasional dinner with someone. I realized that certain aspects of my past with Tiki were absent, but those very things have now come back into my life in real time.

Someone With You...

To confide in
To compliment
To go shopping with
To just sit and listen to
To help make decisions
To know that you can bless them
To do spur-of-the-moment things
To hear them when and if they speak
To laugh with and put a smile on their face
To take pictures of and have theirs taken too
To be around at not quite 24/7, but pretty close
To look into their eyes and have them look back
To just enjoy the moment, the sights, and dinners
To fill the empty seat on the other side of the table
To talk with and ask questions, or sit and be silent
To share their past, pains, thoughts, future hopes,
and to be completely open with.

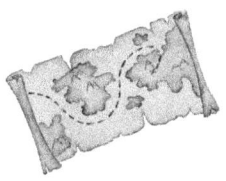

These are just some of the things that reappeared during my trip to Panama City, Panama, to celebrate the coming of a new year. It was a time of reflection to see what was taken from me and what was given back to me for these five days. This was not only about the person I was with, but also about how my outlook on how my future should look. No moments of losing my breath or heart skipping beats, but just a little normalcy back in my life for a short period. Some of these things and situations I've written about in previous writings. Some have changed for the better, and some are still the same. It was a wonderful experience, and maybe it will happen again with her or with someone else. There is no way of knowing what tomorrow and the future will bring into one's life. You never know when someone or something will appear out of the blue. Most of the time, it's when you least expect it and are not looking for it.

January 3, 2025

I wrote these thoughts in my hotel room and on the plane returning to Costa Rica from Panama City, Panama. This was a great experience and an awakening for me.

Sit and Wait

When you just sit back,
To get your life back on track,
Then let them come to you,
So you get a different view.

There's no need to chase
All over the place.
Just sit and look around,
And you just might be found.

There are some who care,
And some who are aware,
Of what you've been through,
And those people may come to you.

Then there are those who come on in,
Who says many words with a spin,
And they have something to say,
That could just make your day,

But don't go out of your way,
And things will be okay,
As you're sitting at home,
Waiting for the unknown.

January 11, 2025

**I wrote this wondering what it would be
like to only sit and wait and see who
shows up in one's life.**

Why?

There is a point in time,
When one thinks all is fine,
But then one comes to see,
Your life's not all it seems to be.

You realize how old you are,
And wonder how you got this far,
Thinking of what you've been through,
And if you are ready for something new?

Should you leave well enough alone,
Or proceed into the unknown?
Not knowing what lies ahead,
Or keep things the same instead?

It's really all up to you.
In whatever you choose to do,
Don't rely on those you know,
Just wake and go with the flow.

You'll always be wondering why,
And your past you can't deny,
So you just take in every new day.
Because your life cannot be replayed.

January 23, 2025

**I wrote this in Destin, Florida, on a day that I
was constantly asking the why questions.
Not the best of feelings on this day.**

If you can't come see me now, please don't bother coming to my funeral. By then, it would be too late, and you would have lost your chance to say goodbye. I don't know what you did or what I did, but whatever it was, it doesn't matter now. Whatever it was, it probably should not have happened. Our lives last for years, and time goes by so fast in this short moment. It's so sad that we could not see eye to eye. But to let you know, I have forgiven you.

January 26, 2025

I wrote this about someone who, for some reason, is very angry with me.

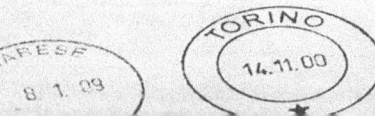

Imagine in the blink of an eye, your house and all your possessions are gone. And now you imagine in the blink of an eye that your spouse is gone too. Both scenarios are very devastating, and even though material things can be replaced, your spouse cannot.

February 2, 2025

Just a thought that came to mind after watching some California fire photos.

Failed Moves

Have you ever seen the vultures fly,
While sitting in a bar getting high,
Two new ladies just walked in—
They're on them and will they win?

Then they offer them their chairs,
Looking to start some new affairs.
Now you listen to their lines,
These guys have developed great designs.

But it doesn't last very long,
Probably from coming on too strong.
Soon the girls move away;
These girls are not quite ready to play.

This was just so fun to watch,
As these guys' plans got botched.
I'm so glad that I'm not right there—
I'm just sitting, watching from my chair.

February 8, 2025

**I'm sitting at Dukes Waikiki Bar in Hawaii, having
a couple of drinks and watching this scene
unfold in front of me. I'm so glad that is
not happening in my life today.**

Who Are They?

Sometimes I wonder if they care
Where I am and if they are aware,
That I'm not who I used to be,
Since I was suddenly set free?

This freedom came with a price;
The present situation is not so nice.
They see I have been left alone,
And now I live life on my own.

It hasn't been an easy thing to do,
Knowing that I haven't had you
With me these past four years.
They know I've shed so many tears.

So now I just drift off to places,
A new world with all new faces.
Who really cares where I stay?
It all comes back to who are they?

February 11, 2025

**I wrote this on the plane from Hawaii back to L.A.
I know whoever "they" are. I normally don't care,
but at times I still wonder which ones "they" are.**

Vacation Living

It's hard to say I'm on vacation,
When I'm in different locations.
I'm living this retired lifestyle,
Only ever staying for a while.

It's always been everyone's dream,
But it's not always what it seems.
My vacations move from place to place,
And everyone I try to embrace.

Each one gives a different view,
Reminds me of those I knew.
Bringing up the things of the past,
Usually with a different cast.

It's hard to compare each of them;
Most of them a special gem.
Some have a special reason,
Or maybe it's just a special season.

But my vacation never ends;
When this one's over the next begins.
This is how I see all nations:
By having back-to-back vacations.

February 16, 2025

**I wrote this at my cousin Steve's house in
Mesa, Arizona, after someone asked if I was
on vacation. I told them I was on a
permanent vacation.**

Crowd Chatter

You're out to dinner all alone,
Sitting within your new safe zone.
There is no one to talk to,
So you choose to listen—listen to who?

Lots of tables that are nearby,
Most of the people you can hear.
Some of them are very loud,
As they talk above the crowd.

But most of them speak in tones,
Keeping their words in their zones.
But if you listen to them all at once,
You wonder what they are all discussing.

Not that you should really care,
For most of them are unaware.
That you can't hear what they say,
But it doesn't matter to me anyway.

It's just another night out,
And I'm still without,
The one that was here.
Why did she disappear?

February 22, 2025

I wrote this sitting at my table alone at B&B Steakhouse in Houston. I always come here the last night before going back to Costa Rica. Nothing has changed.

A Special Song

Was an evening of music and friends,
But it grew a little sad at the end.
To her they dedicated a song,
That's when it didn't take me long—

Not long to feel the thrust in my heart,
Not long to start falling apart.
My breath was taken away,
My feelings I could not delay.

I knew that they loved her so,
Even though she left us long ago.
But to bring her into the show
Was just a way to say hello.

Only a few knew what they'd said,
As I lay here in my bed.
While I wrote down these few lines,
It was one of the many signs.

Signs that she still touches some,
That she can still make me feel numb.
But it's really always nice to know,
You don't always have to let go.

ZZ Top Tribute Band
(John, Tim, & Carl)

February 23, 2025

I wrote this after watching John, Tim, and Carl play
their ZZ Top gig in Ojochal, Costa Rica this evening.
They sang LaGrange and dedicated it to Tiki. I believe
that song had a special meaning from them to her. It
really touched my heart and memories.
Thank you, guys!

SEASON 13:

March 2025 - August 2025

Cliff

Yesterday, we lost a friend,
But his memory will not end.
He was taken by the sea,
Now his soul is set free.

It takes me back four years ago,
When it was me who had to let go.
It was in that very same place—
Those memories time can't erase.

But now once again it starts,
For this family with broken hearts.
The grieving has just begun,
Over the loss of their loved one.

One thing on which we must all agree,
Is that life has no guarantee.
You must take every day as new,
No matter what you have been through.

This family will need their time;
From this valley they will climb.
The hurt won't ever disappear,
Even with family and friends so near.

The special friends will be found,
They will listen and make no sound.
You can open up your heart,
And you can even fall apart.

We shall not forget the one
For whom this poem had begun.
He was a great friend to all,
As many of you will recall.

Cliff & Anna

March 6, 2025

I wrote this in the early hours of this morning
after hearing the news that Cliff from Villa
Lenor lost his life yesterday. His restaurant and
beach held a very special place in my heart—it was
where we held Tiki's memorial service, and where
we shared many great meals and memories with
friends. This is the same place where
he just lost his life. R.I.P.

Sense of Time

At that very first moment
It all started with hours.

Then the hours turned to days.
Days then turned to weeks.
Weeks turned to months.
Now months have turned to years once again.

It has now been four years since you left.
Which is forty-eight months.
Two hundred and five weeks.
One thousand four hundred and sixty-one days.
Thirty-five thousand and sixty-four hours.

But there really is no difference—
In hours, days, weeks, months, or years.
When you've lost the one you love,
They all still seem to be intertwined,
No matter which sense of time,
You are in at that moment.

March 18, 2025

The fourth anniversary of losing Tiki has been on my mind more than usual for the last week or so. I have been jotting down some thoughts, and they all finally came together today. It's four days early, but that's ok. I love and miss you, Tiki.

Decisions

Eventually dealing with the loss,
A line is drawn that I must cross.
Has the time come for something new—
To give myself a different view?

Should I give up what I had,
Even though it will make me sad?
With all the challenges I face,
Should I move to another place?

Sometimes change is for the good;
Other times it's misunderstood.
But maybe it will help me grow,
Is it time for me to let go?

I know I've said this before,
There's a lot out there to explore.
And it's also been said to me,
A permanent place could set me free.

I'd find a place where I'd call home.
But I would still be able to roam.
Somewhat like it used to be,
Before my Tiki left me.

These are thoughts in my head,
A hard decision I dread.
It'd put my life on a new course,
Something new with no remorse.

March 19, 2025

**I had some thoughts about making a change
and trying to be a little more stable in my life.**

Pelican Shadows

I'm just sitting on the beach,
And you are out of my reach.
But I have your urn here,
Because it's been another year.

I have a very empty heart
Since we have been apart.
Time seems to go by so fast,
With all the memories of the past.

Shadows of pelicans for me to see.
Flew on the beach in front of me,
Just like they did four years ago,
So you are here with me I know.

More shadows just flew by,
And I ask myself why?
So now it's happened twice
And it makes this moment nice.

My heart just got refilled,
As the peace in me is fulfilled.
This morning here was meant to be—
Sitting here alone by the sea.

So what can I say?
It's the third time today—
Shadows moving in front of me.
All for me, the only one to see.

March 22, 2025

I wrote this on the fourth anniversary of Tiki's passing. I was
at the beach where we held her memorial service in Costa Rica.
It was a beautiful and peaceful day. As I was writing this,
pelicans flew over and their shadows were on the ground right
in front of me, just like in the video of Tiki's memorial. But this
happened two more times as I was writing this. Could this be a
sign? A reminder of her presence—a gift of comfort.

An Ear Is Near

When you found out they aren't here,
How your loved one has disappeared,
There are so many ways to lose,
In the ways we cannot choose.

There are many ways to go,
It could be very fast or very slow.
There's nothing you can really say,
That will change what happened on that day.

Some of you have time to prepare,
And almost everyone is aware,
That this moment will come.
And your mind will still be numb.

Some we lose in a flash,
Heart attack or a crash.
Or they could pass away in sleep,
No matter how, we will still weep.

It doesn't matter how they left,
It all still feels like a theft.
Something's been taken away from you,
A special person whom you knew.

Now your life is being put to the test.
Don't keep all your thoughts repressed.
Let them out for someone to hear.
There's always a person who will lend an ear.

May 29, 2025

I wasn't sure if I would be able to write anything else or even
if I wanted to after turning in all my writings for this book.
However, I discovered tonight that memories from the past
and current experiences in my life are still surfacing. It's not
just about the loss of a spouse; it is about the loss of just about
anyone. So, I wrote it down and it felt good. I know I am only
one in a million people who are going through
this process of loss.

A Goodbye Kiss

A small kiss happened again.
It just takes me back to when—
When I did the same,
But back then I felt the shame.

But now I can actually see,
Why this kiss was meant to be.
It was a kiss to say goodbye,
And now I want to tell you why.

I just told her I was going away,
And it was hard for me to say.
I didn't want those tears to appear,
It wasn't what she wanted to hear.

But I found out she already knew,
That I just needed to pursue,
My life within this new direction,
To find some kind of reconnection.

Asked what she'd be without,
It was me she was talking about.
She said it was like losing her best friend,
And I didn't quite comprehend.

Been a while since I've had one.
You see, I've just been on the run.
Not getting into anyone's space,
And now you know they're very hard to replace.

August 2, 2025
I wrote this in Costa Rica after telling someone that I was moving back to the U.S.A in December. It was not a comfortable thing to have to do. The truth be told, it made me very sad. But after dinner, as we were leaving, she gave me a memorable kiss. This is the same person and situation that I wrote about in my prose writing titled, "A Kiss."

SEASON 14:

The Final Season

Closure at Candelilla
(Tikivibez)

Sometimes in one's life, you come to a moment when you have to make a big decision. Four days ago, I did just that. I decided that it was time for me to put closure on my life at Candelilla and return to the US in December to live. I've spent nine years here, and it's been four and a half years since I lost Tiki. It's not that I haven't thought about it, written about it, or been urged by others to reflect on it. When I texted my kids, Brianna and Leland, about my decision, they immediately responded with, "Dad, call me now. That is not something you text about."

The next very hard step was to tell Sandy, a very close friend, and John and Janet, my friends to whom I had sold Candelilla to. It was not a very pleasant task for me, and it made my heart ache. But being the true friends that they are, they encouraged me and backed my decision. The few family and friends I have told have all been very supportive, even though I know deep within myself that if they had a choice, they would probably want me to stay in Costa Rica.

There are several reasons that have brought me to this decision. Working with Abigail and Deborah, my publishers, on this book is one. I had no clue that my writings would one day be published. But over the last three months of editing, reading, and rereading them many times over, I think I'm taking a little of my own advice. I've been told by many that I needed to stay longer in places or find a place to call home. I call Costa Rica my home, but I'm only here about every other month and traveling somewhere in the other months. As of this passage, I have no clue as to where I will be going.

This is just the beginning of a new phase of my life. I hope that I can find a place to call home and break free from the "vagabond lifestyle" I've led over the past few years. Also, there might be the possibility of meeting someone to share my adventures with.

What will the future bring? No one knows, and I definitely do not have the answers either.

Candelilla (Tikivibez) in Costa Rica

August 1, 2025

I wrote this at Candelilla (Tikivibez) after deciding to make a life change and move back to the USA. As I've mentioned before, it weighs heavily on my heart, but it's a change I feel is necessary. I will be back!

Family for good reasons...

Friends in all seasons...

Special Thanks To:

John & Janet Chantry
Marco Dittel
Cliff Hubert
&
Michael - The Sand Painter

Your help in organizing the
ceremony and producing
Tiki's video made the day
beautiful and special.
Thank You!

Please take note at the end of the
memorial video, where it states,
"Follow the Son... of God."
This is a testament to Tiki's Savior,
Jesus, and the life that Tiki
led in loving others.

Memorial Ceremony Link:

https://vimeo.com/529799108

Memorial Music:
"I'll Follow the Sun" by The Beatles
Lyrics by John Lennon & Paul McCartney

About the Author
Greg West

Photo Credit: John Konstantaras

Greg West is a man whose life story stretches across continents, decades, and the kind of experiences you can't make up. He was born on an unforgettable date—November 2, 1948, the very day Harry Truman shocked the world with his surprise election victory. Raised in a military family, he grew up traveling across the U.S. and spent three years in France before turning eighteen. That early exposure to change and movement shaped the adaptable, adventurous spirit that defines him today.

After serving four years in the U.S. Air Force and spending his young adult years in Louisiana, Greg eventually found his way to Tyler, Texas, where everything changed. It was there he met Tiki—the love of his life—and her six-year-old daughter Brianna. Together, they built a full and joyful life that included the birth of their son, Leland. They opened a family-run salon, traveled in their motorhome, enjoyed offshore fishing trips, and immersed themselves in decades of laughter, hard work, and duties at church.

As 2016 drew to a close, Greg and Tiki were ready to make some major changes. Leland and Brianna were each successfully and happily married with children of their own. The ups and downs, the stress of deadlines, and the day-to-day responsibilities of dedication and careers in business were over. Tiki closed her hair salon, and Greg retired after twenty-six years. Greg and Tiki took a bold leap in 2017, sold everything, and moved to Costa Rica to enjoy retirement at their special place they had named Candelilla. They embraced the tropical lifestyle, visited their grown children, and soaked in the peace of their new home, until tragedy struck. In March of 2021, Greg lost Tiki after 31 years of marriage. That loss reshaped him again. With the help of family and friends for the first two years, he was just surviving.

Since then, Greg has been on a journey of healing. He sold the property in Costa Rica to close friends who embraced him like family. Though Candelilla has a new name (Tikivibez), he still lives there and calls it home.

Whether exploring in his Sprinter van or flying around the world, Greg now moves with purpose and his phone notes, documenting his thoughts. Writing poetry and reflections about the people and places he encounters has become a meaningful part of his journey. He shares these writings not only as a form of self-expression but also as a way to encourage others walking through life's most difficult seasons.

To the Reader:
I would like to sincerely thank you for taking the time to read my writings. I hope that some of them have touched you. If you know someone this would help, please let them know about this book, or share your copy. Thank You!
—Greg West

To Learn More About Greg's Journey, Follow His Socials:

https://www.facebook.com/authorgregwest
https://www.instagram.com/gregwest1102
Email: AuthorGregWest@gmail.com

About the Publisher

"Weavers of Tales and Tellers of Truth"

Mission Statement:

Our mission is to publish unique and refreshing works from various authors and genres; to present and highlight literary endeavors in an ever-changing marketplace.

Services:

Editing, Formatting, Illustrating, Publishing, Distributing, Local & Social Marketing, Author Coaching

Note to an Author:

Our goal is to walk with you through every step of your publishing journey.

Reach out for a free author consultation:

https://www.pipstones.com/booking-calendar

Enhance your Publishing Journey with Our Newest Book:

Now What?: The 7 Vital Steps to Self-Publish your Manuscript

Now What? Book

Follow our social media for more book news and information:

Facebook: @pipstonespublishing
Instagram: @pipstones
TikTok: @pipstonespublishing
X: @pip_stones